MARTIAL ARTS

SPORTS CHALLENGE

DAVID ARMENTROUT

The Rourke Book Co., Inc.
Vero Beach, Florida 32964

© 1997 The Rourke Book Co., Inc.

David Armentrout specializes in nonfiction writing and has had several book series published for primary schools. He resides in Cincinnati with his wife and two children.

PHOTO CREDITS:
© East Coast Studios: Cover; © Holly Stein/Allsport: page 15; © John Gichigi/Allsport: page 4; © Vandystadt/Allsport: page 16; © R. Tesa/Intl Stock: pages 6, 21; © Bill Stanton/Intl Stock: page 7; © Orion/Intl Stock: page 9; © Westerman/Intl Stock: page 10; © R. Startup/Intl Stock: page 13; © Chad Ehlers/Intl Stock: pages 18, 19; © John Michael/Intl Stock: page 22; © Myrtis & Brack Olds: page 12

EDITORIAL SERVICES:
Penworthy Learning Systems

Library of Congress Cataloging-in-Publication Data

Armentrout, David, 1962 -
   Martial arts / by David Armentrout.
      p. cm. — (Sports challenge)
   Includes index.
   Summary: Presents basic information on the essential skills and techniques for Martial arts.
      ISBN 1-55916-217-1
      1. Martial arts—Juvenile literature. 2. Martial arts for children—Juvenile literature. [1. Martial arts.]
I. Title II. Series: Armentrout, David, 1962 -   Sports challenge.
GV1101.A76 1997
796.8—dc21   97–12421
                                                          CIP
                                                          AC

Printed in the USA

TABLE OF CONTENTS

MARTIAL ARTS

Martial arts include many Asian forms of fighting and self-defense. The use of some martial art forms, or methods, dates back almost 4,000 years. Other forms were not developed until the late 1800's.

Martial arts are enjoyed worldwide by people of all ages. People who practice weaponless martial arts rely on hand blows, foot blows, blocks, throws, and other striking **maneuvers** (muh NOO verz) for self-defense. Some martial arts include weapons like stones, spears, and bamboo swords.

Balance plays a key role in martial arts.

TAKING A CLASS

Martial arts classes are offered in most cities. Professional instructors teach at their own studios and at local gyms and YMCA's.

Instructors from local studios also teach beginner classes at schools. The instructor teaches the basic movements of the art.

Martial arts classes include men and women of different ages.

Wooden sticks are weapons used in some fighting methods.

If the students enjoy their first experience, they can continue with more advanced courses. Becoming an advanced student of the martial arts takes hard work and requires mental discipline.

WARMING UP

Each martial arts class begins with a warm-up session. A warm-up includes special exercises, or **calisthenics** (KAL is THEN iks), that are designed to warm and condition the body.

Some of the exercises work the ankle and knee joints. Others warm and limber the leg muscles. Special push-ups are done to strengthen the arms and shoulders.

Proper physical conditioning helps to prevent muscle and joint injuries and allows the students to perform at their peak.

Martial art exercises are performed daily in this courtyard in China.

KARATE

Karate (kuh RAH tee) may be the most well-known of the martial arts. Karate means "fighting with the empty hand." Karate classes are taught all over the world and attended by people of all ages. Interest in the sport is still growing.

Karate includes punching and kicking maneuvers. Although hand and kick blows are taught, instructors of karate classes also teach protective blocks. Each block is designed to protect a certain area of the body.

Protective blocks are demonstrated by karate experts.

PLAYING HARD

Perfecting the basic karate techniques is called **bunkai** (BOON kye). Each punch, block, and kick has a purpose. Students work hard to learn the meaning of each technique and then practice it over and over.

An instructor teaches and practices with his student.

Two "black belts" demonstrate a judo move.

Form, speed, strength, balance, and timing all play equal roles in karate. They are practiced in an exercise called **kata** (ka TA).

Practice fighting and blocking is both a learning exercise and a fun way to keep in good physical condition.

JUJITSU

Jujitsu (joo JIT soo) is a martial art that was used by Japanese warriors called **samurai** (SAM uh RYE). The warriors used swords when fighting. If the sword was knocked out of his hand, the samurai defended himself using jujitsu movements.

Students of jujitsu practice holds, chokes, throws, and kicks that are meant to stop an attacker. Because they are taught to avoid a fight whenever possible, jujitsu students use their fighting skills only when absolutely necessary.

Boxing and jujitsu experts compete in the ring.

JUDO

Judo (JOO do) is considered a wrestling form of jujitsu. Judo was created by a young Japanese man who wanted people to be able to learn and enjoy martial arts in a safe way.

Like jujitsu, judo techniques are meant to use an attacker's own force against him, or to the advantage of the judo student.

Judo students learn the proper way to weaken an opponent's balance. With the right moves, even a small person can bring down a much taller, heavier attacker.

Judo students use throws to bring down their opponents.

OTHER MARTIAL ARTS

Chinese kung-fu is a 4,000-year-old martial art. Because of its many punching techniques, kung-fu is considered an ancestor of boxing. **Tae kwon do** (TY KWON do) is a Korean martial art that uses lots of kicking.

Sumo wrestlers are presented to the crowd before competition.

Sumo wrestlers prepare to fight.

Sumo wrestling is a popular sport in Japan. Huge men are pitted against each other in a ring. Because kicking and punching are not allowed, pushing, pulling, and slapping are the moves used to force opponents down or out of the ring.

LEVELS, RANKS, AND COMPETITION

There is no standard ranking system for the martial arts, because there are many styles, or schools, for each art. It is common, though, to find beginners wearing white belts and advanced students wearing brown. Black belts are reserved for the experts.

Often, an instructor will promote a student to the next highest rank after a demonstration of skill. Sometimes promotions are awarded only after formal competitions.

Martial art students practice kicks.

GLOSSARY

bunkai (BOON kye) — learning, practicing, and perfecting the basic karate punches, blocks and kicks

calisthenics (KAL is THEN iks) — exercises for developing muscle tone; used as a warm-up in martial arts classes, etc.

judo (JOO do) — a wrestling form of jujitsu

jujitsu (joo JIT soo) — weaponless fighting; "gentleness"

karate (kuh RAH tee) — weaponless fighting; "empty hand"

kata (ka TA) — an exercise used to control and improve strength, balance, form, speed, and timing

maneuvers (muh NOO verz) — movements involving skill and grace

samurai (SAM uh RYE) — a Japanese warrior who fought in a military system that ended in 1871

tae kwon do (TY KWON do) — a Korean fighting system that uses flying kicks and punches

Nunchakus (noon CHA kooz) are weapons used by some martial art experts.

INDEX